FOCUS ON FORMULA ONE

FORMULA ONE TEAMS

BY HEATHER RULE

An Imprint of Abdo Publishing
abdobooks.com

abdobooks.com

Published by Abdo Publishing, a division of ABDO, PO Box 398166, Minneapolis, Minnesota 55439.

Printed in the United States of America, North Mankato, Minnesota.
052023
092023

Cover Photo: Mario Renzi/Formula 1/Getty Images
Interior Photos: Jean-Marc Zaorski/Gamma-Rapho/Getty Images, 4; Bela Szandelszky/AP Images, 7; Attila Kisbenedek/Pool/AFP/AP Images, 9; Bernard Cahier/Hulton Archive/Getty Images, 10; Clive Mason/Getty Images Sport/Getty Images, 13, 15, 29; Hulton Deutsch/Corbis Historical/Getty Images, 16; Stephan Holland/AP Images, 18; Alastair Grant/AP Images, 20–21; Andre Penner/AP Images, 23; Robert Cianflone/Getty Images Sport/Getty Images, 24; Oliver Multhaup/AP Images, 26

Editor: Charlie Beattie
Series Designer: Michael J. Williams

Library of Congress Control Number: 2022949093

Publisher's Cataloging-in-Publication Data

Names: Rule, Heather, author.
Title: Formula one teams / by Heather Rule
Description: Minneapolis, Minnesota: Abdo Publishing Company, 2024 | Series: Focus on formula one | Includes online resources and index.
Identifiers: ISBN 9781098290764 (lib. bdg.) | ISBN 9781098276942 (ebook)
Subjects: LCSH: Formula One automobiles--Juvenile literature. | Automobiles, Racing--History--Juvenile literature. | Sports car racing--Juvenile literature.
Classification: DDC 796.72--dc23

TABLE OF

CONTENTS

Superstar driver Michael Schumacher helped Ferrari dominate Formula One in the early 2000s.

CHAPTER ONE

FERRARI

In his red open-wheel Ferrari Formula One car, Michael Schumacher zoomed through the final laps of the 2000 Japanese Grand Prix. Schumacher crossed the finish line first and slowed on the front straightaway. He pumped both fists in the air to celebrate. Schumacher had just clinched the 2000 Formula One drivers' world championship. He was the first Ferrari driver from the Scuderia Ferrari team—often just called Ferrari—to win a season title in 21 years.

Despite that long winless stretch, the Ferrari Formula One team is one of the most successful in racing history. Ferrari had won 16 world championships through 2022. In July of that year, Charles LeClerc won Ferrari's 242nd race. No other team was even close to 200.

The Formula One world championship started in 1950. Ferrari is the only team that has competed in every season. Argentine José Froilán González brought Ferrari its first race win at the British Grand Prix in 1951. Italian Alberto Ascari won drivers' championships for Ferrari in 1952 and 1953.

TWO WHEELS OR FOUR?

British driver John Surtees won the drivers' championship for Ferrari in 1964. By the time he started his Formula One career, he was already a four-time motorcycle world champion. Surtees was the only man to win world championships on both two wheels and four wheels.

From 2000 to 2004, Ferrari dominated Formula One. The team

Ferrari drivers Rubens Barrichello, *left,* and Schumacher, *second from right,* hold up team principal, Jean Todt, on the podium after taking the top two spots at the 2004 Hungarian Grand Prix.

won both the drivers' and constructors' titles each season. Schumacher won nine races in 2000 on his way to his third championship.

The 2002 season saw Ferrari at its peak. Schumacher finished with 144 points. Teammate Rubens Barrichello added 77 more. The team total of 221 was half the 442 points awarded to Formula One teams that season. Only the Williams BMW team, with 92 points, came even close to competing with Ferrari's dominance. None of the other nine teams had more than 65 points. Two years later, Schumacher won 12 of the first 13 races. He clinched his seventh championship with four races left in the season.

Teams with the most money often do the best on the track. Ferrari has often been an example of that. But the team also had Jean Todt as the team principal in the 2000s. He built a winning culture. Todt often got credit for hiring the right people for the team. One of Todt's key hires was talented racing strategist and technical director Ross Brawn. It was Brawn who handled decisions such as which tires to use and when to bring a car in for a pit stop during a race.

Team Ferrari's crew works on Charles Leclerc's car during a pit stop at the 2022 Hungarian Grand Prix.

After winning a season title in 2008, Ferrari struggled to compete. The team didn't win a single race in 2020 and finished sixth in the constructors' championship. That was Ferrari's lowest finish since 1980. Drivers Leclerc and Carlos Sainz rebounded in 2021 to more than double the team's points the next year.

Mercedes teammates Sterling Moss (10) and Juan Manuel Fangio, *front*, line up before the start of the 1955 Dutch Grand Prix. Fangio won the race while Moss finished second.

CHAPTER TWO

MERCEDES

Lewis Hamilton started in the sixth position for the 2020 Turkish Grand Prix. The Mercedes driver struggled early in rainy conditions, but Hamilton rallied to win the race and claim his record-tying seventh Formula One world championship.

Success for Mercedes goes back to driver Juan Manuel Fangio in the 1950s. He won back-to-back world championships in 1954 and 1955. Mercedes won five times in seven races in 1955 between Fangio and teammate Stirling Moss.

With 27 points to Fangio's 40, Moss finished the year in second place.

However, Mercedes stopped racing activities after the 1955 season. Making race cars required a lot of money and effort. Maintaining a racing team distracted Mercedes from its main business of building cars and engines for everyday drivers. The engineers and mechanics at Mercedes were needed to develop new passenger cars.

ROSBERG WINS AT HOME

Nico Rosberg gave Mercedes its first victory of the 2013 season at the famous Monaco Grand Prix. It was a special moment for Rosberg. He was raised in Monte Carlo, the city in which the race is held. His victory there came exactly 30 years after his father, Keke, won at the Monaco track.

Mercedes didn't race again in Formula One until 2010. The team started off strong with drivers

Lewis Hamilton, *left,* and teammate Nico Rosberg take a corner on their way to finishing first and second, respectively, at the 2014 Spanish Grand Prix.

Nico Rosberg and Michael Schumacher. At least one of them finished in the top 10 in all but one race that season.

At the 2012 Chinese Grand Prix, Rosberg won the team's first pole position since its Formula One comeback. He also won the race. It was the first victory for Mercedes in 57 years.

The next year, Toto Wolff took over as the Mercedes team principal. The wealthy investor transformed the team. One of his biggest moves was signing Hamilton. The then 28-year-old was the sport's hottest driver.

Hamilton and Rosberg dominated, winning a combined 16 of 19 races in 2014. They battled each other for the drivers' championship. Hamilton won 11 races to claim his second world championship, and his first with Mercedes.

Mercedes's hot streak lasted for another seven years. It won eight constructors' titles in a row from 2014 to 2021. Mercedes also took home drivers' titles from 2014 to 2020. Hamilton won six of them. Rosberg won the championship in 2016, with Hamilton finishing second.

Sometimes, an extended period of winning can make a Formula One team lose its edge. Wolff made sure that didn't happen at Mercedes. Wolff also had his team focus on different goals each new season to stay motivated. His honest leadership style and ability to coax performances out of various drivers has helped Mercedes contend every year.

Lewis Hamilton, *left,* poses with Mercedes team principal Toto Wolff after winning his seventh drivers' championship in 2020.

Alain Prost had 30 of his 51 career wins racing for McLaren.

CHAPTER THREE

McLAREN

McLaren's tradition of winning in Formula One goes back to the 1970s. The team had three cars on the track during the 1974 season. Its most consistent driver was Emerson Fittipaldi, who won McLaren its first drivers' title.

However, McLaren was most successful in the 1980s and early 1990s. The team won seven drivers' championships in eight years from 1984 to 1991, along with six constructors' titles. It was usually McLaren teammates competing for championships and creating rivalries. First, Austrian Niki Lauda and Frenchman Alain Prost

Ayrton Senna won titles while racing for McLaren in 1988, 1990, and 1991.

dueled for the 1984 championship. The pair won 12 of the 16 races held that year. Lauda edged out his teammate by half a point for the title. Prost won his first championship a year later, topping second place by 20 points.

Brazilian Ayrton Senna joined McLaren and Prost in 1988. The two drivers were rivals on the track. Both wanted to beat the other. Because of that, McLaren won a lot from 1988 to 1991. McLaren won four constructors' and drivers' titles in a row. Senna won eight of 16 races in 1988 to win the championship as part of a nearly perfect season for McLaren. The team claimed first place in 15 of 16 races. Prost won the title in 1989. Then Senna took the drivers' championships in 1990 and 1991.

The mastermind behind McLaren's dominance was CEO Ron Dennis. He took over the team in

Mika Häkkinen takes the checkered flag at the 2001 British Grand Prix, one of his 20 career victories for McLaren.

1981 and ran McLaren until 2009. In that time, his teams won 140 races. McLaren also won seven constructors' titles during that span.

Dennis continued to have success even after Senna and Prost both left the team in the early 1990s. Dennis brought in Mika Häkkinen in 1993.

The Finnish driver took four years to win a race for McLaren, but more help was on the way.

Dennis hired engineer Adrian Newey away from rival Williams Racing in 1998. Newey was considered one of the best in the sport and had helped Williams win 59 races from 1991 to 1997.

His arrival put Häkkinen over the top. The Finn won 17 of 49 races over the next three years. He was also crowned back-to-back champion in 1998 and 1999.

Nearly a decade after Häkkinen, McLaren brought on another young star. Lewis Hamilton would eventually become best known for his time with Mercedes. But the English driver came into Formula One in 2007 with McLaren. The next year he took home the championship in dramatic fashion. After passing Timo Glock in the final laps of the Brazilian Grand Prix, Hamilton became the sport's youngest champion. He was 23 years old.

Seven years later, McLaren teamed with Honda for its engines. The companies had paired up for a successful run in the 1980s. But this time around, the cars were plagued with reliability issues. Victories were suddenly hard to come by.

Things started to turn for the better in 2021. Drivers Daniel Ricciardo and Lando Norris finished first and second at Monza in Italy. Ricciardo's victory was the first win for a McLaren car in nearly a decade, since 2012.

McLaren driver Lewis Hamilton passes Timo Glock on the last lap of the Brazilian Grand Prix to clinch the 2007 season title.

Red Bull team principal Christian Horner watches on during practice for the 2005 Australian Grand Prix.

CHAPTER FOUR

RED BULL

The Austrian energy drink company Red Bull became a sponsor in Formula One in 1995. In 2004 it bought the struggling Jaguar team from Ford. That purchase started the Red Bull Racing team.

Team principal Christian Horner has guided Red Bull from the start. And a strong business plan helped Red Bull grow quickly. Adrian Newey was hired as chief technical officer in 2006. Newey had been working with championship teams since the early 1990s. Still, critics weren't sure whether Red Bull was serious from the start. When the team

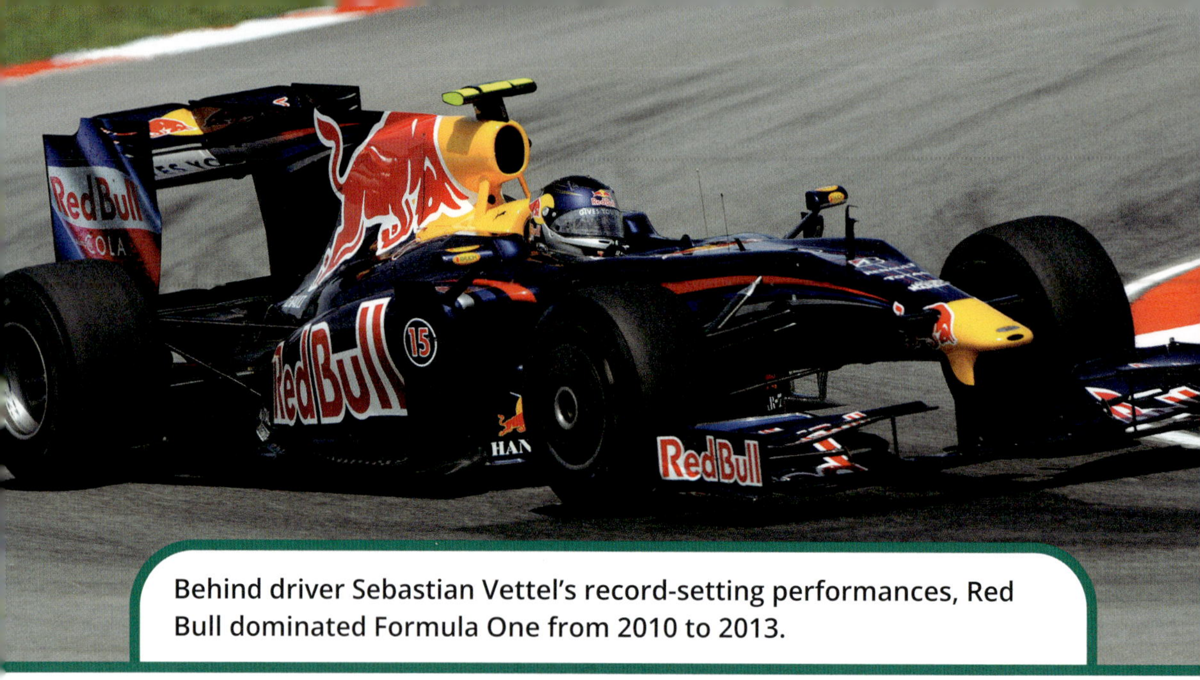

Behind driver Sebastian Vettel's record-setting performances, Red Bull dominated Formula One from 2010 to 2013.

didn't win a race in its first four seasons, many accused the team of simply being a marketing stunt to sell energy drinks.

Everything changed in 2009. That year Formula One changed the rules to even out the aerodynamics of all cars. Red Bull thrived in the new conditions. Its technical team built a winning car. The arrival of young superstar driver Sebastian Vettel also helped. His victory at the 2009 Chinese Grand Prix was Red Bull's first win. Teammate Mark Webber finished second.

A year later, the two drivers competed for the season title. The 23-year-old Vettel won it, starting a four-year run of success for both himself and Red Bull. The German racer topped the standings every year through 2013. Red Bull also won four straight constructors' championships.

Red Bull's dominance ended quickly in 2014. Formula One introduced a new type of engine. Red Bull could not get its Renault-made engines to work reliably. The team struggled through the season and was even worse

OTHER TEAMS

Founded in 1977, Williams Racing has nine world championships and more than 110 total race victories. However, these days it's one of the teams struggling to keep up with the big four. Alfa Romeo, AlphaTauri, Alpine, Aston Martin, and Haas F1 Team were the other teams that competed in the 2022 season.

the next year. Vettel left, and the Red Bull team failed to win any races in 2015.

After several years of difficulty, Red Bull finally reemerged as a power in 2021. Drivers Max Verstappen and Sergio Perez won 11 of the season's 22 races. The Dutch Verstappen claimed his first championship. A year later, Verstappen and Red Bull were even more dominant. Verstappen clinched his second consecutive title with four races to spare.

However, Red Bull's wins were highly criticized. The sport's governing body found that the team spent over the agreed limit for all teams during the 2021 season. Some suggested Verstappen be stripped of his title. Nearly two decades after its founding, Red Bull was still both successful and controversial.

Team Red Bull celebrates after the 2022 Japanese Grand Prix. Driver Max Verstappen, *top,* won the race to clinch his second consecutive season title.

GLOSSARY

chief technical officer
The person who is in charge of a Formula One car's development and makes decisions about a car's technical aspects.

constructors' championship
A title that is awarded each year to the car model that earns the most points throughout the Formula One season.

drivers' championship
A title that is awarded each year to the Formula One driver who earns the most points throughout the racing season.

grand prix
From the French for "grand prize," any race that is part of the Formula One championship series.

open-wheel
Describing a car that has wheels outside the vehicle's main body.

pole position
The most favorable position at the start of an auto race, typically the inside of the front row.

team principal
The person who is in charge of a Formula One team and gives team orders.

MORE INFORMATION

BOOKS

Hustad, Douglas. *Innovations in Auto Racing*. Minneapolis, MN: Abdo Publishing, 2022.

Rule, Heather. *GOATs of Auto Racing*. Minneapolis, MN: Abdo Publishing, 2022.

Stathes, Corbu. *The Best Drivers of Formula One.* Minneapolis, MN: Abdo Publishing, 2024.

ONLINE RESOURCES

To learn more about Formula One teams, please visit **abdobooklinks.com** or scan this QR code. These links are routinely monitored and updated to provide the most current information available.

INDEX

ABOUT THE AUTHOR

Heather Rule is a freelance sports journalist, author, and social media coordinator. She has a bachelor's degree in journalism and mass communication from the University of St. Thomas in St. Paul, Minnesota.